Master Your Emotions

FEELINGS UNDER CONTROL

You Have Everything You Need

ALFRED POTTER

Table of Contents

Chapter 1 Ways To Master Your Emotions 5

Chapter 2: Steps To Choose Mind Over Mood 10

Chapter 3: Stop Worrying and Go To Sleep 14

Chapter 4: How "Lack of Motivation" Has Become A Part of Your Identify and How To Fix It 17

Chapter 5: Ways To Know If You Are A Highly Senistive Person 19

Chapter 6: Ways To Love Yourself First 24

Chapter 7: Ways For Stress Relief 29

Chapter 8: Ways to Cultivate Emotions That Will Lead You To Greatness 33

Chapter 9: Ways To Attract Happiness 38

Chapter 10: Reasons Why Comparison is the Thief Of Joy 43

Chapter 11: Ways Yor Emotions, Thoughts and Behavior Contribute To What's Going On in Your Life 47

Chapter 12: Ways To Transform Your Thinking 52

Chapter 13: Ways To Calm The Emotional Storm Within You 56

Chapter 14: Ways To Get People To Like You 60

Chapter 15: Ways to Define What Is Important In Your Life 64

Chapter 16: Ways to Achieve Peak Performance 69

Chapter 17: Tricks To Become More Aware Of Your Strenghts 73

Chapter 18: Signs You Are Emotionally Unavailable 78

Chapter 19: Reasons Your Emotions Are Getting In The Way of Your Success 82

Chapter 20: Concerning Effects of Mood On Your Life 87

Chapter 21: Ways To Communicate Your Emotional Needs 92

Chapter 22: Scientific Tricks To Become Perfectly Happy 96

Chapter 23: Tips For Mindful Self-Compassion 100

Chapter 24: Five Best Psychological Negotiation Tactics 104

Chapter 1:

6 Ways To Master Your Emotions

As reported by Psychology Today, psychology's answer to the question of "What is emotional mastery?" Has evolved over the last century. Early American psychology embraced the "James-Lange Theory," which held that emotions are strictly the product of physiology (a neurological response to some external stimuli). This view evolved when the "Cannon-Bard Theory" asserted that the brain's thalamus mediates between external stimuli and subjective emotional experience.

The concept of emotional mastery wasn't introduced until the 1960s with the Schachter-Singer experiment, where researchers gave participants a dose of a placebo "vitamin." Participants then watched colleagues complete a set of questionnaires. When the colleagues responded angrily to the questionnaires, the participants felt angry in turn. But when the colleagues responded happily, the participants also felt happy. The study's results implied a connection between peer influence and the felt experience of emotion.

The idea that emotions are influenced by outer as well as inner stimuli was furthered by psychiatrist Allen Beck, who demonstrated that thoughts, peer influence and circumstance shape emotions. Beck's research formed the foundation of modern-day cognitive-behavioral therapy, the gold standard of emotional mastery as it's understood today.

The Role Of Emotional Mastery In Life And Society

Feelings and emotional mastery play a role in our subjective experience and interpersonal relationships.

- **Emotions unify us across cultural lines**. There are six basic emotions that are universal in all cultures: happiness, sadness, fear, anger, surprise and disgust. We all experience these feelings, although there are cultural differences regarding what's an appropriate display of emotion.
- **Emotions govern our sense of well-being**. Since emotions are a product of our experiences and how we perceive those experiences, we can cultivate positive emotions by focusing on them. There are 10 "power emotions" that cultivate emotional mastery by creating a base of positive affect. When we incorporate even small doses of gratitude, passion, love, hunger, curiosity, confidence, flexibility, cheerfulness, vitality and a sense of contribution, we set the stage for feeling good about ourselves.
- **Emotional mastery supports healthy relationships**. When you're able to demonstrate emotions that are appropriate to the situation, you're able to nurture your relationships. When you don't know how to master your emotions, the opposite occurs: You might fly off the handle at minor annoyances or react with

anger when sadness is a more appropriate response. Your emotional response affects those around you, which shapes your relationships for better or worse.

Learning how to master your emotions is a skill anyone can build in six straightforward steps.

1. Identify What You're Really Feeling

The first step in learning how to master your emotions is identifying what your feelings are. To take that step toward emotional mastery, ask yourself:

- What am i really feeling right now?
- Am i really feeling…?
- Is it something else?

2. Acknowledge and Appreciate Your Emotions, Knowing They Support You

Emotional mastery does not mean shutting down or denying your feelings. Instead, learning how to master your emotions means appreciating them as part of yourself.

- You never want to make your emotions wrong.
- The idea that anything you feel is "wrong" is a great way to destroy honest communication with yourself as well as with others.

3. Get Curious About The Message this Emotion is Offering You

Emotional mastery means approaching your feelings with a sense of curiosity. Your feelings will teach you a lot about yourself if you let them. Getting curious helps you:

- Interrupt your current emotional pattern.
- Solve the challenge.
- Prevent the same problem from occurring in the future.

4. Get Confident

The quickest and most powerful route to emotional mastery over any feeling is to remember a time when you felt a similar emotion and handled it successfully. Since you managed the emotion in the past, surely you can handle it today.

5. Get certain you can handle this not only today, but in the future as well

To master your emotions, build confidence by rehearsing handling situations where this emotion might come up in the future. See, hear and feel yourself handling the situation. This is the equivalent of lifting emotional weights, so you'll build the "muscle" you need to handle your feelings successfully.

5. Get Excited and Take Action

Now that you've learned how to master your emotions, it's time to get excited about the fact that you can:

- Easily handle this emotion.
- Take some action right away.
- Prove that you've handled it.

Learning emotional mastery is one of the most powerful steps you can take to create a life that's authentic and fulfilling.

Chapter 2:

3 Steps To Choose Mind Over Mood

Have you ever said something out of anger that you later regretted? Do you let fear talk you out of taking the risks that could really benefit you? If so, you're not alone.

<u>Emotions are powerful</u>. Your mood determines how you interact with people, how much <u>money you spend</u>, how you deal with challenges, and how you spend your time.

Gaining control over your emotions will help you <u>become mentally stronger</u>. Fortunately, anyone can become better at choosing their mind over their mood. Just like any other skill, managing your emotions requires practice and dedication. Managing your emotions isn't the same as suppressing them. Ignoring your sadness or pretending you don't feel pain won't make those emotions go away.

In fact, unaddressed emotional wounds are likely to get worse over time. And there's a good chance suppressing your feelings will cause you to turn to unhealthy coping skills--like food or alcohol. It's important to acknowledge your feelings while also recognizing that your emotions don't have to control you. If you wake up on the wrong side of the bed, you can take control of your mood and turn your day around. If you are angry, you can choose to calm yourself down.

Here are three ways to gain better control over your mood:

1. Label Your Emotions

Before you can change how you feel, you need to acknowledge what you're experiencing right now. Are you nervous? Do you feel disappointed? Are you sad?

Keep in mind that anger sometimes masks emotions that feel vulnerable--like shame or embarrassment. So pay close attention to what's really going on inside of you.

Put a name your emotions. Keep in mind you might feel a whole bunch of emotions at once--like anxious, frustrated, and impatient.

Labeling how you feel can take a lot of the sting out of the emotion. It can also help you take careful note of how those feelings are likely to affect your decisions.

2. Reframe Your Thoughts

Your emotions affect the way you perceive events. If you're feeling anxious and you get an email from the boss that says she wants to see you right away, you might assume you're going to get fired. If however, you're feeling happy when you get that same email, your first thought might be that you're going to be promoted or congratulated on a job well done.

Consider the emotional filter you're looking at the world through. Then, <u>reframe your thoughts</u> to develop a more realistic view.

If you catch yourself thinking, "This networking event is going to be a complete waste of time. No one is going to talk to me and I'm going to look like an idiot," remind yourself, "It's up to me to get something out of the event. I'll introduce myself to new people and show interest in learning about them."

Sometimes, the easiest way to gain a different perspective is to take a step back and ask yourself, "What would I say to a friend who had this problem?" Answering that question will take some of the emotion out of the equation so you can think more rationally.

If you find yourself dwelling on negative things, you may need to change the channel in your brain. A quick physical activity, like going for a walk or cleaning off your desk, can help you <u>stop ruminating</u>.

3. Engage in a Mood Booster

When you're in a bad mood, you're likely to engage in activities that keep you in that state of mind. Isolating yourself, mindlessly scrolling through your phone, or complaining to people around you are just a few of the typical "go-to bad mood behaviors" you might indulge in.

But, those things will keep you stuck. You have to take positive action if you want to feel better.

Think of the things you do when you feel happy. Do those things when you're in a bad mood and you'll start to feel better.

Here are a few examples of mood boosters:

- Call a friend to talk about something pleasant (not to continue complaining).
- Go for a walk.
- Meditate for a few minutes.
- Listen to uplifting music.

Keep Practicing Your Emotional Regulation Skills

Managing your emotions is tough at times. And there will likely be a specific emotion--like anger--that sometimes gets the best of you.

But the more time and attention you spend on regulating your emotions, the <u>mentally stronger</u> you'll become. You'll gain confidence in your ability to handle discomfort while also knowing that you can make healthy choices that shift your mood.

Chapter 3:

Stop Worrying and Go To Sleep

What are we meant to do when we have had a long day and we are finally on our bed but cannot sleep? We cannot let go of all the headaches we go through every day all day long. How can we reset the memories or only the guilt and remorse that we keep carrying each day?

We all want to give up everything for just a good night's sleep, but rarely do we get to enjoy one. We all want everything to be simple and easy for just a short while but, the reality is; we are ready to let go!

I know that life is not a fairy tale and we all have harsh realities that need to be dealt with. But why is that we can't let it get easy even when nothing is wrong in our life?

We are so used to taking pressure that sometimes we feel normal to be so sucked into these unnecessary and unhealthy things. Don't get me wrong, but the pressure is important. Pressure makes you feel like a human and makes us feel like we are the superior of all beings. But staying under the pressure by choice is something that you should never get accustomed to.

Why is it that you are always in need of searching for something that keeps you away from happiness? You have made this false scenario in your head that if everything is wrong and if you close your eyes for just one small moment, everything might turn upside down.

This behavior has spun this emotional roller coaster in us, that does not let us give up on anything even when we are at our lowest.

You have to understand a simple concept. You are an integral part of everyone's life around you. But you are no good to them if you cannot live a long, happy, and healthy life. A life in which you have not dedicated enough time to them, by sharing their feelings and your pain with them.

You need some time off not only for your well-being but indirectly, for them to have you in their lives.

You have to get rid of your past. Get rid of your pains for just a portion of your day or night in that case. Just so you don't seem like a life-less moving object, who talks only when you ask them something.

Be open, be transparent, be indulging, be engaging and be interesting so that you are worth caring for. You cannot expect sympathy and emotions if you are not willing or are not capable of giving something in return.

For that, you need to give your brain some time to shut down and reset. Your brain has an optimal limit to work on its peak, so does your body.

Your body and your brain work in sync to make you look like a proper human being. So don't get in your way to happiness and satisfaction.

So, drop all your anxieties and worries and go to sleep. If you have regrets about doing it, think of it as you are paying back to your body and your loved ones. Paying back for everything that they do to keep you safe and active.

Chapter 4:

How "Lack of Motivation" Has Become A Part of Your Identify and How To Fix It

Do you ever feel when you want nothing to do and nothing to happen to you? You know, when you have had an excellent start to your day, you still don't want things to be more excited. Every now and then, we often have a time when things don't matter to us if they stay the same or don't.
Why is it? Why do we feel so carefree? Why are we so bored when we can be the most exciting person we know?

Many things are going on in everyone's life. I get that. We often get carried away too much in these things, and this is where we want everything to just stop. We want everything to stay put for some time until we are ready for everything to start again.

This is how our lives are now. This is the new norm for most of us. And this is what keeps us from getting to do new things instead of doing nothing at all.

You, me, and many more are stuck in this rut where we don't want to carry on anymore, and we can't afford to give up just now. Upon that, society and the fast track of life keep reminding us that we have to avail our youth to the fullest to reap the fruit peacefully when we are old and curly.

But why does it have to be like this? Who has this proof for such life? A life where you work for fifty years just to live peacefully for twenty-odd ones? It doesn't make any sense!

We all have enforced these false senses of achievements and hopes of a better future when we are not even willing to enjoy our present peacefully. We are so confused with the present and the future that we are not ready to give into anything. We just want to opt-out. And this feeling of wanting to let go is what's causing us to drop hard.

So what can you do to indulge in your emotional self and look out for the good things in life? It is easy and straightforward as the question. Start off by making a list of everything you want to do. Write down your priorities and make a specific time for those.

Don't go all our working on those things only. You work for a said time, and then, you are free to do whatever you want. No matter if it is just sleep that you need or a friendly company that nurtures you as a human. Talk to those people and spill your heart out. The ones who love you will never shrug you off but will always make you feel possessive and empowered within yourself, and this is what will keep your demotivation away. You only need one good person to motivate you, and if that person isn't someone else, it is undoubtedly within yourself!

Chapter 5:

9 Ways To Know If You Are A Highly Sensitive Person

Being highly sensitive is personality trait that some of us may possess. Some people are born with it and some people are shaped by their life experiences, but whatever the reason is, it's there.

Barring all the articles and videos that you will find out there on this topic, my definition of a highly sensitive person is someone who has heightened emotions and sensitivity to the world around them. He or she is also a person highly driven by feelings and of the heart rather than the mind.

If you feel that you may be a highly sensitive person but aren't sure, we are going to explore today how we can identify the signs and traits of this unique personality. We will also address how you can manage your emotions when people come across too strong for your liking.

Here are 9 Ways To Know if You're A Highly Sensitive Person

1. You Pick Up On Subtle Emotional Cues

If you're a highly sensitive person, it is most likely that you're in tune with physical cues that regular people won't necessarily pick up on. Whether it is through someone's facial expression, your inner intuition towards an unfamiliar person, or picking up hints that someone is unhappy with you even though they try to hide it very well. Being highly sensitive allows you to have a strong radar and 6th sense on these things. More often than not, you are usually right on the money.

2. Other People's Tone Is Very Important To You

If someone's tone sets you off easily, you may be a highly sensitive person without realizing it. Tonality is very important to you, and you get easily put off when someone doesn't speak to you in quite the right way. Other people might have to be very careful when communicating with you and that could be a problem in relationships if people don't understand that side of you. Communicate to others that you may be offended without meaning it, but that you will just need some time to get past it if they are unknowingly triggering you in some ways.

3. You Are Driven By Intense Emotions

Does watching a sad movie make you cry but others around you don't? Or do you feel incredibly over-the-top happy while others around you simply feel like it was just alright? If you are a highly sensitive person, it is most likely that intense emotions are what drives you. You feel the extreme end of the spectrum. You may cry your eyes out in happiness or sadness, and that's perfectly fine. Embrace your feelings and don't change anything about you.

4. You Tend To Withdraw When Things Get Too Much To Handle

When things get incredibly overwhelming, do you feel a need to just crawl away and hide instead of facing the problem head on? When we are driven my intense emotions, sometimes it can work against us. We may feel bulks of sadness and fear that paralyses us from doing anything. If that is you, considering working through these emotions one step at a time and break down the problem you face into smaller chunks.

5. You Think Deeply About Things

If you have a tendency to question about life and your existence on this earth, you may be a highly sensitive person. As you are more in tuned with the world and the mind, inevitably philosophy will be something that you will naturally gravitate towards. Entertain these thoughts and express yourself in ways that celebrate your uniqueness.

6. People And Activities Drain You

If hanging out with large groups drain you more than they energise you, or if people's problems are not something that you can handle, you may be highly sensitive. Absorbing all the energy from others can be a very exhausting experience. If you need to, take a step back and spend time alone to recharge your batteries before putting yourself out there again.

7. There's No Middle Ground

You either feel incredibly happy or incredibly sad, there's no middle ground when it comes to your emotions. You either feel happy to be around someone or you just simply want to avoid them like the plague, you don't have the patience or tolerance to perform niceties to people you feel ambivalent about.

8. You Always Feel Misunderstood

Being highly sensitive could mean that you always feel that people don't understand you or are actually hearing what you say, even if in actual fact that they are and do. You always feel a need for reassurance and double confirmation that everything is heard loud and clear. Don't fall into the trap of having to over-defend your position on something if someone doesn't seem to see eye to eye on you on certain matters. It usually isn't their fault.

9. You Love Nature More Than People

Being around other humans can be exhausting for you if you absorb and feed off their energy all the time. Sometimes nature is one that actually revitalised and recharges you. You feel at home with the birds and the trees, the tranquility, and the peace that nature brings to you. Take time out of your schedule to visit the beach, parks, and gardens energise you and release all the built up emotions that other humans and dumped on you.

Chapter 6:

8 Ways To Love Yourself First

"Your task is not to seek for love, but merely to seek and find all the barriers within yourself that you have built against it." - Rumi.

Most of us are so busy waiting for someone to come into our lives and love us that we have forgotten about the one person we need to love the most – ourselves. Most psychologists agree that being loved and being able to love is crucial to our happiness. As quoted by Sigmund Freud, "love and work … work and love. That's all there is." It is the mere relationship of us with ourselves that sets the foundation for all other relationships and reveals if we will have a healthy relationship or a toxic one.

Here are some tips on loving yourself first before searching for any kind of love in your life.

1. Know That Self-Love Is Beautiful

Don't ever consider self-love as being narcissistic or selfish, and these are two completely different things. Self-love is rather having positive regard for our wellbeing and happiness. When we adopt self-love, we see higher levels of self-esteem within ourselves, are less critical and harsh with ourselves while making mistakes, and can celebrate our positive qualities and accept all our negative ones.

2. Always Be Kind To Yourself

We are humans, and humans are tended to get subjected to hurts, shortcomings, and emotional pain. Even if our family, friends, or even our partners may berate us about our inadequacies, we must learn to accept ourselves with all our imperfections and flaws. We look for acceptance from others and be harsh on ourselves if they tend to be cruel or heartless with us. We should always focus on our many positive qualities, strengths, and abilities, and admirable traits; rather than harsh judgments, comparisons, and self-hatred get to us. Always be gentle with yourself.

3. Be The Love You Feel Within Yourself

You may experience both self-love and self-hatred over time. But it would be best if you always tried to focus on self-love more. Try loving yourself and having positive affirmations. Do a love-kindness meditation or spiritual practices to nourish your soul, and it will help you feel love and compassion toward yourself. Try to be in that place of love throughout your day and infuse this love with whatever interaction you have with others.

4. Give Yourself a Break

We don't constantly live in a good phase. No one is perfect, including ourselves. It's okay to not be at the top of your game every day, or be happy all the time, or love yourself always, or live without pain. Excuse your bad days and embrace all your imperfections and mistakes. Accept your negative emotions but don't let them overwhelm you. Don't set high standards for yourself, both emotionally and mentally. Don't judge yourself for whatever you feel, and always embrace your emotions wholeheartedly.

5. Embrace Yourself

Are you content to sit all alone because the feelings of anxiety, fear, guilt, or judgment will overwhelm you? Then you have to practice being comfortable in your skin. Go within and seek solace in yourself, practice moments of alone time and observe how you treat yourself. Allow yourself to be mindful of your beliefs, feelings, and thoughts, and embrace solitude. The process of loving yourself starts with understanding your true nature.

6. Be Grateful

Rhonda Bryne, the author of The Magic, advises, "When you are grateful for the things you have, no matter how small they may be, you will see those things instantly increase." Look around you and see all the things that you are blessed to have. Practice gratitude daily and be thankful for all the things, no matter how good or bad they are. You will immediately start loving yourself once you realize how much you have to be grateful for.

7. Be Helpful To Those Around You:

You open the door for divine love the moment you decide to be kind and compassionate toward others. "I slept and dreamt that life was a joy. I awoke and saw that life was service. I acted, and behold, and service was a joy." - Rabindranath Tagore. The love and positive vibes that you wish upon others and send out to others will always find a way back to you. Your soul tends to rejoice when you are kind, considerate, and compassionate. You have achieved the highest form of self-love when you decide to serve others. By helping others, you will realize that you don't need someone else to feel complete; you are complete. It will help you feel more love and fulfillment in your life.

8. Do Things You Enjoy Doing

If you find yourself stuck in a monotonous loop, try to get some time out for yourself and do the things that you love. There must be a lot of hobbies and passions that you might have put a brake on. Dust them off and start doing them again. Whether it's playing any sport, learning a new skill, reading a new book, writing in on your journal, or simply cooking or baking for yourself, start doing it again. We shouldn't compromise on the things that make us feel alive. Doing the things, we enjoy always makes us feel better about ourselves and boost our confidence.

Conclusion:

Loving yourself is nothing short of a challenge. It is crucial for your emotional health and ability to reach your best potential. But the good news is, we all have it within us to believe in ourselves and live the best life we possibly can. Find what you are passionate about, appreciate yourself, and be grateful for what's in your life. Accept yourself as it is.

Chapter 7:

8 Ways For Stress Relief

From minor to major issues, stress is naturally part of life. Even when the current circumstances have highlighted the rising stress levels, the phenomenon is not new. And while you may have no control over your circumstances, you control how you react to them. Stress can gravely take a toll on your overall health if it becomes chronic or overwhelming. In fact, according to a study that was conducted in 2012, unmanaged daily stress increases the likelihood of developing chronic health problems 10 years down the road.

So, is stress becoming more infuriating and upsetting? Is it affecting your mental peace and overall healthy? Relieving your daily stress is the most pleasing way of restoring serenity and calmness. Simply put, resort to the following easy, and proven stress relief techniques.

Here are 8 ways for stress relief.

1. Log Off, Stay Unplugged

Relieving stress is possible by simply pressing the "turn off" button on your phone. In the same efforts you put to control your diet, do the same to your social media interactions especially in the first hour of your day. Take command of the first hour by clearing your mind, setting motives, stretching, and hydrating. Doing so allows you to gain clarity and control of the entire day.

2. Take Charge

One of the primary causes of stress is losing control over one's circumstances. Taking control is an empowering act in and of itself, and it's a necessary step toward finding a solution that calms you down. Every issue has a solution. And if you remain passive, blaming yourself for being in that situation, you are in for the worst.

3. Exercise

Although exercising cannot erase all your stressful thoughts permanently, it will help you relieve the intensity and thus allowing you to handle the problems more calmly. In a recent Medicine and Science in sports and exercise journal, exercising is found to be the most accurate and healthy way of dealing or relieving stress. The journal suggests moderate physical exercises like running, dancing, and spinning as stress relievers.

4. Resort to Healthy Drinking and Eating Lifestyle

To cope with stress, we frequently turn to excessive alcohol or overeating. Yes, these habits are relaxing in the short term, but they increase stress in the long haul. Furthermore, they will degrade your health. Instead, resort to a healthy eating and drinking plan.

5. Try Something New

Establishing new goals or challenging yourself, such as learning a foreign language, volunteering, or participating in a sport, can enable you to build confidence. You also lower or relieve tension while participating in such activities. Continued learning makes you a more emotionally resilient person. It equips you with knowledge and motivates you to act rather than sit back and just do nothing.

6. Leave the Work-Life at Your Office

A person who can leave their professional life at the office to savor their personal life can effectively deal with daily stress. Strike a work-life balance and mindset whereby both are adding value to your life. Don't be a person whose career defines who you are.

7. Accept Change

Change is never easy to accept or incorporate into one's daily life. And changing a problematic situation that you've found yourself in isn't easy. However, to move forward positively and avoid becoming entangled in that situation, you must accept change. The goal is to avoid wasting time on things that drain your energy and make you unhappy because you need to be productive and add value to your life. Just prioritize things you are in control of and leave the rest to Mother Nature.

8. Laugh More Often

Having a moment where you feel a good sense of humor won't take your pain away, but it will make you feel better. Laughter alleviates stress and causes profound positive effects on the body. It stimulates and deactivates the stress response. So, you can embark to good Netflix comedies, or hang out with funny friends.

Conclusion

Life is full of inevitable ups and downs, and it's all normal to experience stress at all walks of your life. To maintain your sanity, you'll need to bring down stress to a manageable level. Apply the above stress relief strategies at every stage of your life.

Chapter 8:

7 Ways To Cultivate Emotions That Will Lead You To Greatness

Billions of men and women have walked the earth but only a handful have made their names engraved in history forever. These handful of people have achieved 'greatness' owing to their outstanding work, their passion and their character.

Now, greatness doesn't come overnight—greatness is not something you can just reach out and grab. Greatness is the result of how you have lived your entire life and what you have achieved in your lifetime. Against all your given circumstances, how impactful your life has been in this world, how much value you have given to the people around you, how much difference your presence has made in history counts towards how great you are. However, even though human greatness is subjective, people who are different and who have stood out from everyone else in a particular matter are perceived as great.

However, cultivating greatness in life asks for a 'great' deal of effort and all kinds of human effort are influenced by human emotions. So, it's safe to say that greatness is, in fact, controlled by our emotions. Having said that, let's see what emotions are associated with greatness and how to cultivate them in real life:

1. Foster Gratitude

You cannot commence your journey towards greatness without being grateful first. That's right, being satisfied with what you already have in life and expressing due gratitude towards it will be your first step towards greatness. Being in a gratified emotional state at most times (if not all) will enhance your mental stability which will consequently help you perceive life in a different—or better point of view. This enhanced perception of life will remove your stresses and allow you to develop beyond the mediocrity of life and towards greatness.

2. Be As Curious As Child

Childhood is the time when a person starts to learn whatever that is around them. A child never stops questioning, a child never runs away from what they have to face. They just deal with things head on. Such kind of eagerness for life is something that most of us lose at the expense of time. As we grow up—as we know more, our interest keeps diminishing. We stop questioning anymore and accept what is. Eventually, we become entrapped into the ordinary. On the contrary, if we greet everything in life with bold eagerness, we expose ourselves to opportunities. And opportunities lead to greatness.

3. Ignite Your Passion

Passion has become a cliché term in any discussion related to achievements and life. Nevertheless, there is no way of denying the role of passion in driving your life force. Your ultimate zeal and fervor towards what you want in life is what distinguishes you to be great. Because admittedly, many people may want the same thing in life but how bad they want it—the intensity of wanting something is what drives people to stand out from the rest and win it over.

4. Become As Persistent As A Mountain

There are two types of great people on earth 1) Those who are born great and 2) Those who persistently work hard to become great. If you're reading this article, you probably belong to the later criteria. Being such, your determination is a key factor towards becoming great. Let nothing obstruct you—remain as firm as a mountain through all thick and thin. That kind of determination is what makes extraordinary out of the ordinary.

5. Develop Adaptability

As I have mentioned earlier, unless you are born great, your journey towards greatness will be an extremely demanding one. You will have to embrace great lengths beyond your comfort. In order to come out successful in such a journey, make sure that you become flexible to unexpected changes in your surroundings. Again, making yourself adaptable first in another journey in itself. You can't make yourself fit in adverse situations immediately. Adaptability or flexibility is cultivated prudently, with time, exposing yourself to adversities, little by little.

6. Confidence Is Key

Road to greatness often means that you have to tread a path that is discouraged by most. It's obvious—by definition, everybody cannot be great. People will most likely advise against you when you aspire something out of the ordinary. Some will even present logical explanations against you; especially your close ones. But nothing should waver your faith. You must remain boldly confident towards what you're pursuing. Only you can bring your greatness. Believe that.

7. Sense of Fulfilment Through Contributions

Honestly, there can be no greater feeling than what you'd feel after your presence has made a real impact on this world. If not, what else do we live for? Having contributed to the world and the people around you; this is the purpose of life. All the big and small contributions you make give meaning to your existence. It connects you to others, man and animal alike. It fulfills your purpose as a human being. We live for this sense of fulfillment and so, become a serial contributor. Create in yourself a greed for this feeling. At the end of the day, those who benefit from your contributions will revere you as great. No amount of success can be compared with this kind of greatness. So, never miss the opportunity of doing a good deed, no matter how minuscule or enormous.

In conclusion, these emotions don't come spontaneously. You have to create these emotions, cultivate them. And to cultivate these emotions, you must first understand yourself and your goals. With your eye on the prize, you have to create these emotions in you which will pave the path to your greatness. Gratitude, curiosity, passion, persistence, adaptability and fulfillment—each has its own weight and with all the emotions at play, nothing can stop you from becoming great in the truest form.

Chapter 9:

7 Ways To Attract Happiness

We have seen a lot of people defining success as to their best of knowledge. While happiness is subjective from person to person, there's a law of attraction that remains constant for everyone in the world. It states that you will indirectly start to attract all the good things in life when you become happier. This is why happy people often have good lives where everything just somehow tends to work for them. Happiness not only feels good but can also make our manifestation attempts twice as effective. We shouldn't measure our happiness from external factors but instead, as cliche as it may sound, we should know that true happiness comes from the inside.

Here are some ways for you to attract happiness:

1. Make a Choice To Be Happy

When you choose to be as happy as you can in every moment of your life, your subconscious mind will start acknowledging your decision, and it will begin to find ways to bring more joy into your life. When you work towards your decision of being happy, the universe also plays its part and makes sure it attracts more situations in your life that you can be pleased about. The positive vibrations that you will give out will find their way back to you. You don't have to make the decision of being happy right away, as some of you might be going through a tough time. Sit, relax, and take some time to reflect on yourself first and then make a choice whenever you're ready.

2. Define What Happiness Means To You

We have also found ourselves asking this question a million times, "what exactly is happiness?" Some people would attach the idea of happiness with materialistic things such as a big house, expensive cars, branded clothes and shoes, designer bags, the latest technologies, and so forth. While for some, happiness is merely spending time with family and friends, doing the things that they love, and finding inner peace and calm.

3. React Positively Under All Situations

We could experience a thousand good things but a million bad ones in our everyday lives. And sometimes, it could be complicated for us to encounter any kind of happiness given the circumstances. Although these circumstances cannot be in our control, how we react to them is always in our hands. As our favorite Professor Dumbledore once said, "Happiness can be found even in the darkest of times if only one remembers to turn on the light." Similarly, we should always try to find that silver lining at the end of the dark tunnel, always seek some positivity in every situation. But we are only humans. Don't try to enforce positivity on yourself if you don't feel like it. It's okay to address all our emotions equally till you be yourself again.

4. Do Not Procrastinate

You might find it a bit weird, but procrastination does snatch your happiness away. No matter how much things are going well in your life, you would always find a loophole, a reason to be unhappy and dissatisfy with yourself a well as your life. Procrastination makes you believe that you are not living up to your fullest potential. You will get this nagging feeling that will eventually morph into negative emotions that would nearly eat you. So, try to avoid procrastination as much as possible and start doing the things that actually matter.

5. Stay Present

The key to becoming more focused, more at peace, more effective in manifesting, and eventually, much happier is to just live in the moment. Whatever you're doing in the present, try to be completely aware and focused on it. It will help you avoid all the negative feelings you have conjured up about the past and future. Try to stay present as much as you can; over time, it will become a habit, and you will develop the capability to face it all. This will definitely help you attract more happiness into your life.

6. Do Not Compare Yourself

As Theodore Rosevelt once said, "Comparison is the thief of joy." Whenever we compare ourselves to others, we tend to become ungrateful and strip ourselves of the ability to appreciate the good and abundance in our lives. We start to magnify the good in other people's lives and the bad that is in our own. We must understand that everyone is going through their own pace, and they all are secretly struggling with one thing or the other.

7. Don't Try Too Hard

Happiness demands patience. It is better to get into it gradually rather than being overeager. Many people take the law of attraction and being positive a little too far and start obsessing over it. They tend to panic if they get negative thoughts or are unable to attract the things they want. Don't get frustrated if things don't work out your way, and don't give up on the idea of happiness if you feel distressed. Try to prioritize your happiness and give others a reason to be happy too. Make yours as well as other's lives easy.

Conclusion:

Not many people know that but being happy is actually the foundation towards attracting all your dreams and goals. When you adopt the habit of becoming truly happy every day, everything good will naturally follow you. Over time, happiness can even become your default state. Try your best to follow the guidelines above, and I guarantee that you will start feeling happier immediately.

Chapter 10:

7 Reasons Why Comparison is The Thief of Joy

Comparison is a poison that creates feelings of jealousy and envy if we do not put reframe our pattern of thought. It is perfectly natural for us to engage in the habit of comparing our lives with those around us even if we had no business to do so.

When we scroll through social media or hear stories of friends who have bought multi-million dollar properties, it's hard not to look at your own life and wonder what went wrong. Chasing other people's life even though they are not yours can only lead to nowhere.

Today we are going to find out 8 reasons why comparison is the ultimate thief of joy and happiness in our lives.

1. Feelings of Unworthiness

When we engage in comparisons with people who have fancy houses and cars, or those who have very successful careers, especially if they are friends of ours, it is hard not to feel sorry for ourselves. We feel inadequate and lacking. This inferiority complex only serves to remind us that we are lousy and useless, rather than the truth that we are special, unique, and amazing human beings who deserve to be respected and treated the same as people who are 1000x more successful than we are. No amount of success and wealth should make you feel unworthy in the presence of others.

2. We Feel Like We Are Not Where We Should Be

Comparing the amount of stuff and the level of career progression is not something that we should indulge in. That person we are comparing against may have some special talents, are gifted in areas of making money, or whatever reasons that landed them their position today, but that doesn't mean they are better than you. We are all on our own journeys - as long as we are on a path that we have set for ourselves, no matter how unglamorous it is, it is one that we should be proud of.

3. We Constantly Envy Others

Envy is not a good emotion to have, especially if it only makes us bitter at our life circumstances. We start blaming the things around us, our parents, our environment, and so on for the lack of success that we supposedly feel that we should have by now. There will always be someone richer and more successful than you, if you are never happy at where you are, you will never be really happy at all.

4. We Forget How Amazing Our Life Is

Engaging in comparisons is a sure-fire way to help us forget how amazing our lives are. Suddenly everything you you own feels like trash next to someone who has something fancier. Your trusty Toyota feels like a garbage vehicle next to a Bentley, your nice condo suddenly feels like a mouse-hole next to that giant bungalow, and your well-to-do income suddenly seems like pocket money next a multi-million-dollar earner. Always remind yourself that your life is amazing and that there are people in third world countries who are living life in poverty without proper food and shelter. You are living their dream life.

5. We Try To Force Our Way Into The Life That Others Are Living

By wanting what others have, you may have the tendency to copy their way of life. To try and emulate others, you are abandoning your own beliefs, goals, and dreams, to chase someone else's. You may attempt to climb that same mountain but you may never feel as happy as you are right now doing what you do for a lot less money and stress. People are all wired differently. Some may be workaholics who are able to spend 14 hours a day at the office while not caring about everything else in their life. Are you able to do the same? And are your priorities in life the same as well? If the answer is no, stick to your own path and be happy in it.

6. We Fail To Be Grateful For What We Have

It is perfectly easy to forget how grateful we should be to be alive. That we are born on this earth, and we are gifted an opportunity to explore, create, and live. We fail to be grateful for the family and family in our lives, instead looking at the missing pool in our backyard or that extra zero in our bank accounts. Money can be earned, and things can be bought, but family and friends only come once in your life. Don't forget you have all these things the next time you compare yourself with someone else.

7. We Are Never At Peace

We all want to have peace of mind. To be able to rest one day on our deathbed and say we have lived a great life. If even in our golden years, we are comparing ourselves with our peers who have achieved fancier things in life, we may only look back in life in regret rather than wonder. Don't waste your time comparing, instead celebrate and live each day in the present.

Conclusion

Focus on yourself. Focus on your journey. Focus on your own path to success. That is the only way forward that you should be striving for. You will be much happier for it. Be thankful that you can walk this earth and pursue your dreams. All will fall into place in time. I believe in you.

Chapter 11:

6 Ways Your Emotions, Thoughts, and Behavior Contribute To What's Going On In Your Life

Emotions, thoughts, and behavior have an impact to compel us to do certain things in life. They control what we chose to do and what we don't. Sometimes it drives us to the significant ability to perceive and believe. It also forces us towards the outlook of the specific state of affairs. The emotion and thoughts we process while being conscious are easy to change and modify.

Somehow, emotions, thoughts, and behavior are interconnected with each other in a way or another. They depend on one another. The specific concept of an idea drives us towards a particular emotion. That emotion then leads us to the formation of different behaviors or actions. So, therefore, we can say that these turns on each other contribute to our lives. We depend on them on a daily basis.

1. The Benefits of Positive and Negative Emotions

We experience lots of emotions in our single life, either positive or negative. Positive emotion drives us to the more elite type of happiness, and it can make us aware of the bright side of everything. We feel light and satisfactory by almost the whole lot. Positive emotion opens our minds to more probability and prospects.

However, Negative emotions are just as important. The unconscious feeling of being alert and attentive saves us from trouble sometimes. But, a good balance of negative and positive emotions is needed in life to keep steadiness and right footing.

2. Emotion Intuition and Remembrance

A simple potion of positive emotion can encourage us to push ourselves more in some aspects of life, like studying for an exam or preparing for an interview. It can help us with the confidence of proving ourselves academically and educationally. The need to be successful and being on top comes with positive emotion to do so. It operates our intellect in such a way that we consider favorable outcomes in almost every facet. It intensifies the power of remembrance and enhancing our memory to a great extent. Even a negative emotion helps us to study because we become attentive due to the fear of losing or failing in that department. So, emotion does play an important role academically.

3. The Importance of Good Thoughts

We think about every action we imply beforehand. We are constantly analyzing everything in our brain before the consequence, even unconsciously sometimes. The thoughts drive us to specific behavior we carry out in our standard of living. As we have already imagined the outcome before the accurate results, we get a sense of comfort for what will happen. We become more relaxed and at ease. However, thinking too much or too excessively can be substandard for us and our mental health. Then over time, it becomes difficult to shut our mind when needed, which causes the formation of negative thoughts, which become, comparatively, more than the positive thoughts we had. Thus, we always need to relax our minds occasionally.

4. Thinking About Making The Decision

Making a decision can sometimes be a hard choice. The idea of choosing an option between two or more always seems quite strenuous. The fear of choosing the wrong or the comfort of choosing right comes with a great deal of moderate thought over the situation. So, we always give our thoughts a run at the circumstances, that what can be the outcome of a particular choice we are making in the process. Our thoughts constantly survey the position we are put into. We always get indecisive at some point, As it becomes difficult to concentrate on rights and wrongs. We would always need the thought of a master plan to a wiser choice.

5. The Welfare of Good Behavior

The behavior tells a lot about a person. Their personality depends upon the actions they manifest in daily life and all aspects of living. Good emotion and thought lead to good behavior. The action speaks louder than the words, so the behavior applied to the circumstance should be according to the requirement of the situation. It plays a vital role in daily life as we have to go through it daily to contribute to life. The power of influence nowadays is wielded like a weapon to build the strength of controlling specific points.

6. To Infuse Time and Energy

The public nowadays requires a working or waging method that uses the least amount of time and energy. Laziness has become a more prominent feature of society. A person's actions need more attention and energy to go through certain things, which makes it difficult for a person to ignore by time. There is a need to observe the gaps in certain situations and invest their time to get to the bottom of complex conditions. The men become determined to resolve such cases. It gives it all its time and energy to contribute to the simple necessities of life. And by the end of the day, the work can be done by multiple methods through observation.

Conclusion

Our emotions, thoughts, and behavior contribute in almost every way in our lives. Whether it be a positive thought, negative emotion, or excessive behavior, we always need them to complete our lifestyle by a large fraction. One impact each other, so the calculation to perform even a simple task needs work in these three aspects daily.

Chapter 12:

6 Ways To Transform Your Thinking

Changing your mindset isn't easy, but an open and positive attitude. Personal growth contributes to our choices to achieve physical, emotional, and spiritual well-being. Even something as simple as changing your mind can change your life. It's essential to take time for your mindset. During this period, we begin to understand ourselves, making us more compassionate and patient with ourselves. Our societies and cultures thrive in the professions that life brings to our lives and our tables. In this regard, the use of "bandage" solutions and rapid remedies to overcome certain obstacles in our lives have implications. These decisions never last long and are a matter of time and effort to slow down, ground up, and shift focus. Changing your mind means becoming more optimistic and giving your mind the breathing space, it needs to grow and expand. It's about looking at everything that doesn't work for you and being open to other methods that might help.

1. Practice Mindfulness

To adopt a more positive mindset, you must first recognize your current mindset. As you develop mindfulness, you can recognize and identify habituated thought patterns and then decide whether to use them or not. Mindfulness creates a distance between you and your thoughts, allowing you to see yourself separate from them. Incorporate mindfulness into your morning or evening routine and sit quietly for a few minutes (and practice gradually increasing the amount of time). When a thought comes to mind, turn your attention to your breathing instead of clinging to it.

2. Address Your Inner Critic

Your inner critic likes to convince you that it's not true, which often makes you feel pretty bad. Think of this voice as separate from you. Challenge the lie he is trying to feed you. Ask yourself. Is it true? Is there any evidence to support this claim? Another way is to thank this inner voice for their opinion and then say "no." I prefer not to fall into these negative thoughts. Alternatively, you may choose shorter, more direct answers, such as Not Now or Delete.

3. Know Your Triggers

It is essential to be aware of certain people, situations, and situations to trigger more negative thoughts. Meeting your boss or making important life decisions can make you overly critical of yourself or question your worth. Once you become aware of your triggers, you can better prepare to control your thoughts than go back to your old negative thinking patterns. It is also helpful to see which cognitive biases, such as those mentioned above, recur most often.

4. Write It Out

Writing down your feelings on paper is a great way to relieve your thoughts and learn more about them. We often don't realize how harmful our thoughts are. Negative thinking patterns become habitual over time and usually go unnoticed. Taking notes makes it easier to identify areas that need attention. You can also ask questions as soon as they appear in the article to ensure they are accurate and relevant. If not, let them go or replace them with more positive thoughts. Writing in a diary, the first thing you do when you wake up in the morning is the perfect time to write down your stream of consciousness on paper.

5. Recite A Mantra

Shouting out a mantra or positive affirmation is a great way to break free from your current negative thoughts. When you feel that something negative is coming, you can make it a habit to recite or focus on it several times throughout the day. You can choose words or phrases that remind you to focus on the present and focus more on the positive.

6. Change Your Surroundings

Sometimes the thoughts are so loud that it is best to change the physical environment. Go for a walk, run or meet friends in nature. The point is to engage in something other than a negative cycle so you can get back to the problem when you're in a cleaner space. Choose your favourite activity or place, and you will feel better. If you need to be with others, have people around you to encourage you to think positively. (Avoid the trigger!)

Negative stereotypes of thoughts are challenging to break, especially when habituated. Patterns that have existed for years don't disappear overnight, so it's essential to show compassion and patience for yourself as you work.

Chapter 13:

3 Ways To Calm The Emotional Storm Within You

When emotions are already intense, it's often hard to think about what you can do to help yourself, so the first thing you need to work on is getting re-regulated as quickly as possible. Here are some fast-acting skills that work by changing your body's chemistry; it will be most helpful if you first try these before you're in an emotional situation, so you know how to use them.

1. Do A Forward Bend

This is my favourite re-regulating skill. Bend over as though you're trying to touch your toes (it doesn't matter if you can actually touch your toes; you can also do this sitting down if you need to, by sticking your head between your knees). Take some slow, deep breaths, and hang out there for a little while (30 to 60 seconds if you can). Doing a forward bend actually activates our parasympathetic nervous system – our 'rest and digest' system – which helps us slow down and feel a little calmer. When you're ready to stand up again, just don't do it too quickly – you don't want to fall over.

2. Focus On Your Exhale With 'Paced Breathing'

It might sound like a cliché but breathing truly is one of the best ways to get your emotions to a more manageable level. In particular, focus on making your exhale longer than your inhale – this also activates our parasympathetic nervous system, again helping us feel a little calmer and getting those emotions back to a more manageable level. When you inhale, count in your head to see how long your inhale is; as you exhale, count at the same pace, ensuring your exhale is at least a little bit longer than your inhale. For example, if you get to 4 when you inhale, make sure you exhale to at least 5. For a double whammy, do this breathing while doing your forward bend.

These re-regulating skills will help you to think a little more clearly for a few minutes, but your emotions will start to intensify once more if nothing else has changed in your environment – so the next steps are needed too.

3. Increase Awareness of Your Emotions

In order to manage emotions more effectively in the long run, you need to be more aware of your emotions and of all their components; and you need to learn to name your emotions accurately. This might sound strange – of course you know what you're feeling, right? But how do you know if what you've always called 'anger' is actually anger, and not anxiety? Most of us have never really given our emotions much thought, we just assume that what we think we feel is what we actually feel – just like we assume the colour we've always called 'blue' is actually blue; but how do we really know?

Sensitive people who have grown up in a pervasively invalidating environment often learn to ignore or not trust their emotional experiences, and try to avoid or escape those experiences, which contributes to difficulties naming emotions accurately. Indeed, anyone prone to emotion dysregulation can have trouble figuring out what they're feeling, and so walks around in an emotional 'fog'. When you're feeling 'upset', 'bad' or 'off', are you able to identify what emotion you're actually feeling? If you struggle with this, consider each of the following questions the next time you experience even a mild emotion:

- What was the prompting event or trigger for the feeling? What were you reacting to? (Don't judge whether your response was right or wrong, just be descriptive.)

- What were your thoughts about the situation? How did you interpret what was happening? Did you notice yourself judging, jumping to conclusions, or making assumptions?

- What did you notice in your body? For example, tension or tightness in certain areas? Changes in your breathing, your heart rate, your temperature?

- What was your body doing? Describe your body language, posture and facial expression.

- What urges were you noticing? Did you want to yell or throw things? Was the urge to not make eye contact, to avoid or escape a situation you were in?

- What were your actions? Did you act on any of the urges you noted above? Did you do something else instead?

Going through this exercise will help you increase your ability to name your emotions accurately. Once you've asked yourself the above questions, you could try asking yourself if your emotion fits into one of these four (almost rhyming) categories: mad, sad, glad, and afraid. These are terms I use with clients as a helpful starting point for distinguishing basic emotions, but gradually you can work on getting more specific; emotions <u>lists</u> can also be helpful.

Chapter 14:

6 Ways To Get People To Like You

We are always trying for people to like us. We work on ourselves so that we can impress them. Everyone can not enjoy a single person. There will always be someone who dislikes them. But, that one person does not stop us from being charming and making people like us. In today's generation, good people are difficult to find. We all have our definition of being liked. We all have our type of person to select. That makes it very hard for someone to like someone by just knowing their name. We always judge people quickly, even to understand their nature. That makes it hard to like someone.

People always work their selves to be liked by the majority of people. It gives you a sense of comfort knowing that people are happy with you. You feel at ease when you know that people around you tend to smile by thinking about you. For that, you need to make an excellent first impression on people. Training yourself in such a way that you become everyone's favorite can sure be tiring. But it always comes with a plus point.

1. Don't Judge

If you want people to like you, then you need to stop judging them. It is not good to consider someone based on rumors or by listening to one side of the story. Don't judge at all. We can never have an idea of what's going on in an individual life. We can not know what they are going through without them telling us. The best we can do is not judge them. Give them time to open up. Let them speak with you without the fear of being judged. Assuming someone is the worst without you them knowing is a horrendous thing to do.

2. Let Go of Your Ego and Arrogance

Make people feel like they can talk to you anytime they want. Arrogance will lead you nowhere. You will only be left alone in the end. So, make friends. Don't be picky about people. Try to get to know everyone with their own stories and theories. Make them feel comfortable around you to willingly come to talk to you and feel at ease after a few words with you. Being egotistic may make people fear you, but it will not make people like you. Be friendly with everyone around you.

3. Show Your Interest In People

When people talk about their lives, let them. Be interested in their lives, so it will make them feel unique around you. Make sure you listen attentively to their rant and remember as much as possible about a person. Even if they talk about something boring, try to make an effort towards them. If they talk about something worth knowledge, appreciate them. Ask them questions about it, or share your part of information with them, if you have any on that subject. Just try to make an effort, and people will like you instantly.

4. Try To Make New Friends

People admire others when they can click with anyone they meet. Making new friends can be a challenge, but it gives you confidence and, of course, new friends. Try to provide an excellent first impression and show them your best traits. Try to be yourself as much as possible, but do not go deep into friendship instantly. Give them time to adapt to your presence. You will notice that they will come to you themselves. That is because they like being around you. They trust you with their time, and you should valve it.

5. Be Positive

Everyone loves people. You give a bright, positive vibe. They tend to go to them, talk to them and listen to them. People who provide positive energy are easy to communicate with, and we can almost instantly become friends. Those are the type of people we can trust and enjoy being around. Positivity plays a critical role in your want to be liked. It may not be easy, but practice makes perfect. You have to give it your all and make everyone happy.

6. Be Physically and Mentally Present For The People Who Need You

People sometimes need support from their most trusted companion. You have to make sure you are there for them whenever they need you. Be there for them physically, and you can comfort someone without even speaking with them. Just hug them or just try to be there for them. It will make them feel peaceful by your presence. Or be there emotionally if they are ready. Try to talk to them. Listen to whatever they have to say, even if it doesn't make sense. And if they need comfort. Try to motivate them with your words.

Conclusion

You need to improve yourself immensely if you want people to like you. Make sure you do the right thing at the right time. Make people trust you and make them believe your words. Even a small gesture can make people like you. Have the courage to change yourself so that people will like you with all their heart's content.

Chapter 15:

6 Ways To Define What Is Important In Your Life

In this crazy world that we live in, the course of evolution spirals upward and downward, and the collective humanity has witnessed glorious times and horrific ones. The events around us change minute-to-minute. So much seems out of our control, but we find solace in knowing that one thing remains within our immediate control; taking back ownership and responsibility for ourselves. If life has gotten away from you and you feel overwhelmed, anxious, or depressed, then maybe it's time to stop and refocus on what's most important to you and find a way back to what really matters to you.

The idea is to evaluate what you're actually doing with and for yourself, determine if it's even essential to you, and then make the said necessary changes that will best accommodate your needs, interests, and desires. Here are some ways to consider how and on what things you should refocus your attention to determine what is most important in your life.

1. Determine What Things You Value Most

Choose and focus on the things around which you have to structure the life that you want to create. When you consciously make these choices, you are more focused on reminding yourself what things in your life you can't and won't do without. These all represent the backbone of your life. We often forget that people and events play a massive role in shaping up to our lives. They Mold us into what we have become so far and what we are to become in the future. Their support and encouragement in our lives are undeniable. We have to see which people and what events we value the most in our lives and then should keep our focus on them more.

2. Decide What Commitments Are Essential To You

Keeping the above valuable things in mind, evaluate which commitments do you value the most in your life. Commitments are the obligations you enter into willingly and represent your promise to see any relationship/project/contract conclusion steadfastly. Renegotiate your essential commitments, if necessary, but consider completing the existing commitments that you are already obligated to and refuse to take any new ones if you aren't ready. That way, you will focus more and fulfill those commitments first that are more significant to you and your life.

3. Assess The Way You Use Your Time

Most of us have a fixed daily routine, with many fixed activities, habits, and chores. Evaluate which things are absolutely necessary and vital for shaping up your life and yourself daily. Assess the time you spend communicating, how much of your time you spend online, emailing, texting, or on your cell phone. How can you cut back the amount of time spent on these activities to do something more productive? How much time are you spending on TV, radio, reading newspapers and magazines? Consider decreasing your consumption and receive the basic information from a reputable source only once throughout the day. Avoid repetition and redundancy.

4. Get Rid of Any clutter That's In Your Life

Look around you and see, do you need everything you have? Give away anything that you haven't used since the last two years. It could be anything, from selling items to furniture, clothing, shoes, etc. Anything that you no longer need. Someone else can happily use what you haven't all this time. And not just the worldly things; get rid of all the emotional and psychological clutter you have kept aside for so long, and it no longer serves you. We have to get rid of the old things to make room for the new things to come. This will help us reflect on our actual being of who we are and where we are.

5. Spend More Time With People That Matter To You

Evaluate how much quality time you actually spend with your family and close friends. As life evolves, more people will enter into your sphere. These people may fall into different categories of importance in your life, such as acquaintances, colleagues, friends, partners, etc. Our time is precious, so it is wise to use it on those that matter to us the most. It's necessary to sort out our interactions and to assess the meaning of each relationship to us.

6. Make Time To Be Alone

It all comes down to how much time do you make yourself at the end of the day? What was the last time you spent doing something you're passionate about or what you love doing? Give yourself all the time and permission to express your creativity and make peace with your mind. Take care of your body, spirit, and mind because these are the things that will make you feel alive. Take a walk and look around, reacquaint yourself with all the beauty around you. Make each breath count.

Conclusion

Identifying and understanding your values is a challenging but as well as an essential exercise. Your personal values are a central part of defining who you are and who you want to be. By becoming more aware of these significant factors in your life, you can use them as your best guide in any situation. It's comforting and helpful to rely on your values since most of our life's decisions are based on them.

Chapter 16:

6 Ways To Achieve Peak Performance

To be successful requires much more than just your intelligence and talent. There are basic needs which have to be met to function at your peak. These basic needs are neglected by most, impairing their capacity to rise to those elusive higher levels of success and happiness in life.

1. Get Enough Sleep

Sleep deprivation means peak performance deprivation. Without proper sleep you wake up to meet the day feeling scatterbrained, foggy and unfocused. You grab your cup of coffee to get a charge on your brain, which completely depletes your brain function over the course of the day, making your brain even more exhausted.

Good sleep improves your ability to be patient, retain information, think clearly, make good decisions and be present and alert in all your daily interactions. Sleep is your time off from problem solving.

When you get the proper rest your brain becomes awake, alive and ready to generate the cognitive prowess and emotional regulation you need to function at your peak performance.

2. Drink Lemon Water

Lemon water is a great substitute for your morning coffee. Although lemons do not contain caffeine, lemon water has excellent pick-me-up properties without negative side effects. It energizes the brain, especially if it is warm, and hydrates your lymph system.

Among the most important benefits of lemon water are its strong antibacterial, antiviral, and immune-boosting power, making sick days from work nearly non-existent. Lemon water cures headache, freshens breath, cleanses the skin, improves digestion, eliminates PMS with its diuretic properties and reduces the acidity in the body.

Most importantly, lemon water increases your cognitive capacity and improves mood with its stimulating properties on the brain, helping you to operate more consistently in your peak performance zone.

3. Get Daily Exercise

Exercise is the best way to reduce the stress that impairs your performance stamina. Exercise increases your "happy" mood chemicals through the release of endorphins. Endorphins help rid your mind and body of tension alleviating anxiety helping you to calm down.

The brain needs physical activity to stay flexible. Exercise stimulates neurogenesis, or the growth of new brain cells, which improves overall brain function. The development of new brain cells keeps your brain young and in shape, allowing you to be more efficient, pliable and clear in your decision making, higher thinking and learning capacities. Neurogenesis is the catalyst to peak performance.

Further, there is nothing that can bring down self-esteem quicker than not liking how you look. Exercise improves self-confidence and your perception of your attractiveness and self-worth. This confidence contributes greatly to your success, prompting people to respect you and take you seriously

4. Have Emotional Support

Having healthy, loving relationships increases your happiness, success and longevity by promoting your capacity to function in life as your best self. Social connectedness and love gives you relationships to be motivated for and people to be inspired by.

A strong social network decreases stress, provides you with a sense of belonging and gives your life the deeper meaning it needs. When you are loved and loving, and carving out quality time to cultivate these relationships, you are exalted, elevated and encouraged to live your dreams fully.

5. Be Unapologetically Optimistic

A requirement of peak performance is to look for the best in every situation. Optimism is the commitment to believe, expect and trust that things in life are rigged in your favor. Even when something bad happens, you find the silver lining.

A positive outlook on life strengthens your immune system and the emotional quality of your life experiences, allowing you to be resilient in the face of fear, stress and challenge.

Being an optimist or a pessimist boils down to the way you talk to yourself. When you are optimistic you are fierce in the belief it is your own actions which result in positive things happening. You live by positive affirmation, take responsibility for your own happiness and anticipate more good things will happen for you in the future.

When bad things happen you do not blame yourself, you are simply willing to change yourself.

6. Have Time Alone

Time alone is refueling to your physical, mental, emotional and spiritual self. This time recharges you, helping to cultivate your peak performance levels again and again. You must give yourself time to recover from the stress of consistently being around others. Being around people continuously wears down your ability to regulate your emotional state, causing self-regulation fatigue. For this reason you must give yourself permission to take the pressure off and disconnect.

Chapter 17:

6 Tricks To Become More Aware Of Your Strengths

"Strength and growth come only through continuous effort and struggle." - Napoleon Hill.

While it is true that we tend to focus more on our weaknesses than on our strengths, it is also true that we should polish our strengths more than our weaknesses. This in no way means that we should consider ourselves superior to others and start looking away from that we have flaws. Unfortunately, most of us don't spend much time on self-reflection and self-awareness. But they are the vital aspects if we are thinking of improving ourselves in any way.

Here are 6 Tricks to become more aware of your strengths:

1. Decide To Be More Self-aware

Human beings are complicated creatures. Our minds are designed so that we tend to absorb more negative than positive thoughts about ourselves and others. For this reason, self-awareness is perhaps the most crucial thing in an individual's life. Self-awareness is the ability to look deep inside of yourself and monitor your emotions and reactions. It is the ability to allow yourself to be aware of your strengths, weaknesses, as well as your triggers, motivators, and other characteristics. We'll help you find a set of tricks and techniques that you can apply to polish your strengths in a self-awareness way; and how to use your strengths in a promising way.

2. Meditation

The first thought that will come to your mind would be, "Is this person crazy? How can meditation help us improve our strengths?" But hear me out. The fresh breeze of the morning when everything is at peace, and you sit there inhaling all the good energy in and the bad energy out, your mind and thoughts would automatically become slow-paced and calm. Once you get to relax with yourself, you can analyze the things that have been happening in your life and develop possible solutions on how you can deal with them using your strengths. The positive energy and calming mood you will get after meditating would help you make your decisions wisely when you are under pressure and your mind is in chaos.

3. Labelling Your Thoughts:

More often, our thoughts reflect on our behavior and what makes us fail or succeed in life. People can genuinely relate to a situation where they could have possibly thought about a worst-case scenario, but in the end, nothing as such happened. Our anxiety and hopelessness don't come from the situation we are struggling with, but rather our thoughts make us believe in the worst possible things that could happen to us. But we're stronger than we give ourselves credit for. We have the power to control our negative thoughts and turn them into positive ones. We can list all the ideas and thinking that provide us with stress and tension and then label them as either useful or useless. If the particular thought is causing a significant effect in your life, you can work towards it to make your life better and less anxious. Know your priorities and take help from your strengths to tackle the problems.

4. Befriending Your Fears

There's not a single person on this planet who isn't afraid of something. Be it the fear of losing your loved ones or any phobias of either animal, insects, heights, closed spaces, etc. There are also so many fears related to our self-worth and whether we are good enough, skilled enough, or deserving enough of anything. To accept these fears and work towards overcoming them is perhaps the most powerful thing one could do. It takes so much of a person's strength and willpower to befriend fear, reduce it, and finally eliminate it. Most of the time, we end up in situations that we always feared, and then we have to take quick actions and make wise decisions. To remain calm in such cases and use your strengths and experiences to tackle whatever's in front of you is a remarkable quality found in only a few. But we can also achieve and polish this quality by strengthening our minds and preparing ourselves to get us out of situations wisely and effectively. To be patient and look into the problems from every angle is the critical component of this one.

5. Watching Your Own Movie

Narrating your life experiences to yourself or a close friend and telling yourself and them how far you have come can boost your self-confidence immensely. You should go in flashbacks and try to remember all the details of your life. You will find that there were some moments you felt immense joy and some moments where you felt like giving up. But with all the strength that you were collecting along the way, you endured the possible tortures and struggles and challenges and eventually rose again. So you should focus and be well aware of how you tackle those situations, what powers you have, and the strengths that couldn't let you give up but face everything. Once you have found the answers to the above questions, like for example, it was your patience and bravery that helped you through it, or it was your wise and speedy decisions that made it all effective, you can understand what strengths you have and make use of them later in life too.

6. Motivate Yourself

We should stop looking for others to notice how great we did or stop waiting for a round of applause or a pat on the back from them. Instead, we should motivate ourselves every time we fall apart, and we should have the energy to pick ourselves back up again. The feeling of satisfaction we get after completing a task or helping someone, that feeling is what we should strive for. We should become proud of ourselves and our strengths, as well as our weaknesses, that they helped us transform into the person we are today. We should never feel either superior or inferior to others. Everyone has their own pace and their own struggles. Our strengths should not only be for ourselves but for others too. Kindness, empathy, hospitality, being there for people, patience, courage, respect are all the qualities that one must turn into their strengths.

Conclusion

The key to perfection is self-awareness. There's a fine line between who you are and who you strive to become; it can be achieved by becoming aware of your strengths, polishing them, and creating a sense of professional as well as personal development. Your strengths motivate you to try new things, achieve new skills, become a better version of yourself. Your strengths are what keeps you positive, motivated, help you to maintain your stress better, aid you in your intuitive decision making, and command you to help others as well. It inspires you to become a better person.

Chapter 18:

6 Signs You Are Emotionally Unavailable

In times of need, all we want is emotional comfort. The people around us mainly provide it. But the question is, will we support them if the need arises? You might be emotionally unavailable for them when they need you. It is necessary to have some emotional stability to form some strong bonds. If you are emotionally unapproachable, you will have fewer friends than someone you stand mentally tall. It is not harmful to be emotionally unavailable, but you need to change that in the long run. And for that, you need to reflect on yourself first.

It would help if you always were your top priority. While knowing why you are emotionally unapproachable, you need to focus on yourself calmly. Giving respect and talking is not enough for someone to rely on you. You need to support them whenever needed. Talk your mind with them. Be honest with them. But not in a rude way, in a comforting way. So, next time they will come to you for emotional support and comfort. If you are relating to all these things, then here are some signs that confirm it.

1. You Keep People At A Distance

It is usual for an emotionally unavailable person to be seen alone at times. They tend to stay aloof at times; that way, they don't have to be emotionally available. And even if you meet people, you always find it challenging to make a bond with them. You might have a few friends and family members close to you. But you always find meeting new people an emotionally draining activity. You also might like to hang out with people, but opening up is not your forte. If you are emotionally unavailable, then you keep people at a hands distance from you.

2. You Have Insecurities

If you struggle to love yourself, then count it as a sign of emotional stress. People are likely to be unavailable emotionally for others when they are emotionally unavailable for themselves too. We always doubt the people who love us. How can they when I, myself, can't? And this self-hatred eventually results in a distant relationship with your fellow beings. Pampering yourself time by time is essential for every single one of us. It teaches us how one should be taken care of and how to support each other.

3. You Have A Terrible Past Experience

This could be one of the reasons for your unapproachable nature towards people. When you keep some terrible memory or trauma stored inside of you, it's most likely you cannot comfort some other being. It won't seem like something you would do. Because you keep this emotional difference, you become distant and are forced to live with those memories, making things worse. It would help if you talked things out. Either your parents or your friends. Tell them whatever is on your mind, and you will feel light at heart. Nothing can change the past once it's gone, but we can work on the future.

4. You Got Heartbroken

In most cases, people are not born with this nature to be emotionally unavailable. It often comes with heartbreak. If you had a breakup with your partner, that could affect your emotional life significantly. And if it was a long-term relationship, then you got emotionally deprived. But on the plus side, you got single again. Ready to choose from scratch. Instead, you look towards all the negative points of this breakup. Who knows, maybe you'll find someone better.

5. You Are An Introvert

Do you hate going to parties or gatherings? Does meeting with friends sound tiresome? If yes, then surprise, you are an introvert. Social life can be a mess sometimes. Sometimes we prefer a book to a person. That trait of ours makes us emotionally unavailable for others. It is not a bad thing to stay at home on a Friday night, but going out once in a while may be healthy for you. And the easiest way to do that is to make an extrovert friend. Then you won't need to make an effort. Everything will go smoothly.

6. You Hate Asking For Help

Do you feel so independent that you hate asking for help from others? Sometimes when we get support from others, we feel like they did a favor for us. So, instead of asking for help, we prefer to do everything alone, by ourselves. Asking for aid, from superior or inferior, is no big deal. Everyone needs help sometimes.

Conclusion

Being emotionally unavailable doesn't make you a wrong person, but being there for others gives us self-comfort too. It's not all bad to interact with others; instead, it's pretty fun if you try. It will make your life much easier, and you will have a lot of support too.

Chapter 19:

6 Reasons Your Emotions Are Getting In The Way Of Your Success

Do you ever ponder on why your new year's resolutions fail miserably? It is primarily because of the toxic emotions and our negative thoughts of the past that keeps us stuck with the same patterns and regrets. We can try to change and manage our attitudes well, but the emotions are out of our hands. So even though we can't control what we feel, we must confront them to achieve our goals and resolutions.

A therapist in Tarzana, California, Vicki Botnick, explains that any emotion – even elation, joy, or others you would typically view as positive – can intensify to a point where it becomes difficult to control.

Here are 6 Reasons why emotions are getting in the way of your success

1. You Let Your Emotions Rule You

Most of us are clueless about taking control of our emotions and how they affect our productivity. But we must manage them if we strive to achieve our goals. Emotions are an instant response to a specific trigger. All of our emotions are interlinked with each other. For example, we can't taste the satisfaction of joy if we don't go through any pain, or we can't enjoy courage without being fearful first. All of these emotions are what make us human. Embracing both negative and positive emotions are essential, but if they start to get in the way of your success, then you must take action and act upon them.

2. Anger

"The greatest remedy for anger is a delay." - Thomas Paine.

Anger is the majorly common emotion that humankind feels. This negative emotion can result from frustrations, conflicts, mistreatment, or interpersonal conflicts, or is sometimes triggered by an event or experience that happened in the past. For example, suppose you studied really hard for a test but didn't get the expected grade. The next time when you're willing to give it another try, you won't study as much as you did the first time because you'll remember your previous failed attempt. You will re-live your failure and will eventually become frustrated and demotivated. The best thing to do in this scenario is just to take some time off and breathe. Distance yourself from everything and get yourself to calm down before making any decision. Ask yourself then, are you too hard on yourself? Are you trying to do everything at once that's causing you to get upset? Have you set the bar too high? Ponder on these questions and then look for the solutions calmly. Being angry about the things you can't control is pointless, as anger feeds more anger, and you would get stuck in an endless loop of resentment and frustration. Seek solutions on the things you can control and be patient.

3. Fear

The fear of failure is perhaps the worst emotion we can endure. It snatches away even the slightest chance of taking that first step to achieving our dreams and goals. The reasons why we are so afraid of failures may vary from person to person. Some people can't digest that they are full of flaws and that failure is the most crucial step towards leading a successful life. They want to win no matter what. Others might feel that they are not good enough if they can't achieve something. Most people don't admit that they have fears. Fear can either be your greatest friend or your worst enemy; it all depends on how you treat it, whether you look into its eyes and face it or run from it. Living fearlessly doesn't mean that a person isn't afraid of anything, but rather that the person has befriended his fears and is now dancing with them. One shouldn't run away from the challenges that the world throws at him, but stand up to them bravely and face them. Make a list of all the things that scare you or are distracting you from achieving your goals. And then work towards them until they no longer bother you or gets in the way of your success. A famous African proverb states, "Smooth seas do not make skillful sailors."

4. Envy

Bertrand Russell once said, "Beggars do not envy millionaires, though of course, they will envy other beggars who are more successful." Envy and jealousy are the two strongest emotions that mankind has experienced. Although they go hand in hand with each other, there is still a slight difference between them. Being envious wants the other person's things, while jealousy wants the other person's recognition from others. Whenever things tend to go south, we start to become envious of those who are successful. We compare ourselves to them, idealize their successes, and in the process, we lose ourselves. We shift our focus from our signs of progress to being demotivated and stressed out. Pain is an indicator of progress. When we stretch our minds beyond our comfort zone, we feel pain. This pain is the indication that we should move forward and not run away. We shouldn't compare our initial progress to those who have been striving for years. Everyone has their own pace. We should focus on ourselves and setting our potentials free.

5. **Guilt**

The guilt of doing something else or saying something else instead of what you already did or said will forever haunt us. Guilt gets us stuck in the past rather than live in the present moment. There is a term in psychology, The Zeigarnik Effect, which refers that people remember uncompleted tasks more than the completed ones. They then blame themselves for not doing it sooner or better. Our mindset is often linked with productivity blame, where we feel bad for achieving something or not working hard enough. We tend to punish ourselves emotionally and get the idea that we can never reach our goals. But it is essential to take some time off and treat yourself with kindness and empathy. Don't over-pressurize yourself. Self-appreciate and become a better version of yourself in the process. "Mistakes are always forgivable if one dares to admit them." - Bruce Lee.

6. Sadness

"We must understand that sadness is an ocean, and sometimes we drown, while other days, we are forced to swim." - R.M. Drake.

Feeling sad or low on energy crushes productivity and enthusiasm. We feel demotivated and can't focus on our tasks. Sadness makes us feel secluded and isolated. We must embrace this emotion at our own pace, but we shouldn't hide away from whatever it is that's bothering us. Start again slowly with your productivity, make slight progress, start rechallenging yourself. But don't do all of this unless you feel okay again.

Conclusion

Understanding how your emotions are getting in the way of your productivity requires practice. Self-awareness is the key to know yourself better, so you can deal with your emotions efficiently. Please pay close attention to what your feelings are trying to tell you rather than running away from them.

Chapter 20:

6 Concerning Effects of Mood On Your Life

By definition, mood is the predominant state of our mind which clouds over all the other emotions and judgements. Our mood represents the surface-level condition of our emotional self.

Mood is very versatile and sensitive. Subtle changes in our surroundings or even changes in our thoughts directly affect mood. And consequently, our mood, being the leader of our mental state, affects us, as a whole—even impacting our life directly.

Take notes of these following points so that you can overpower your mood and take complete control of your life.

Here Are 6 Ways How Changes In Your Mood Can Impact Your Life:

1. Mood On Your Judgement and Decision-Making

Humans are the most rational beings—fitted with the most advanced neural organ, the brain. Scientists say that our brain is capable of making one thousand trillion logical operations per second and yet still, we humans are never surprised to make the stupidest of judgements in real life.

Well, along with such an enormous 'Logical reasoning' capacity, our brains also come with an emotional center and that is where mood comes in to crash all logic. Most of the decisions we make are emotional, not logical. Since our emotions are steered by mood, it is no surprise that we often make irrational decisions out of emotional impulses.

But again, there are also some instances where mood-dictated decisions reap better outcomes compared to a logical decision. That's just life.

2. Mood Affects Your Mental Health

While our mood is a holistic reflection of our mental state caused by various external and internal factors, it is also a fact that our mood can be the outcome of some harboring mental illness. Both high degree of euphoria and depression can be an indication of mood disorder—just on two opposite ends of the spectrum.

There is no specific cause behind it except that it is a culmination of prolonged mood irregularities. And mood irregularities may come from anywhere i.e., worrying, quarrelling, drug abuse, period/puberty, hormonal changes etc. If such mood irregularity persists untreated, it may deteriorate your overall mental health and result in more serious conditions. So, consider monitoring your mood changes often.

3. Correlation Between Mood and Physical Well-Being

We have heard the proverb that goes, "A healthy body is a healthy mind". Basically, our body and mind function together. So, if your body is in a healthy state, your mind will reflect it by functioning properly as well. If on the other hand your body is not in a healthy state, due to lack of proper nutrition, sleep, and exercise, then your mind will become weak as well. Yes, according to research, having a persistent bad mood can lead to chronic stress which gradually creates hormonal imbalance in your body and thus, diseases like diabetes, hypertension, stroke etc. may arise in your body. Negative moods can also make you go age faster than usual. So having a cheerful mood not only keeps you happy but also fuels your body and keeps you young. Aim to keep your body in tip top condition to nourish the mind as well.

4. Effect Of Your Mood On Others

This is obvious, right? You wouldn't smile back at your significant other after you have lost your wallet, spilled hot coffee all over yourself and missed the only bus to your job interview.

Your mood overshadows how you behave with others. The only way to break out of this would be to meditate and achieve control over your emotional volatility—believe that whatever happened, happened for a reason. Your sully mood doesn't warrant being hostile with others. Instead, talk to people who want the best of you. Express your griefs.

5. Mood As A Catalyst In Your Productivity

Tech giants like Google, Apple, Microsoft all have certain 'play areas' for the employees to go and play different games. It is there to remove mental stress of the employees because mood is an essential factor in determining your productivity at workplace. According to experts, people with a negative mood are 10% less productive in their work than those who are in a positive mood. This correlation between mood and productivity is an important thing to be concerned about.

6. Mood Change Your Perspective

Everyone has their own point of view. Perspectives of people vary from individual to individual and similarly, it varies depending on the mood of an individual. On a bad day, even your favorite Starbucks drink would feel tasteless. It doesn't mean that they made a bad drink—it means that you're not in the mood of enjoying its taste. So, how you perceive things and people is greatly affected by your mindset. Pro-tip: Don't throw judgement over someone or something carrying a bad mood. You'll regret it later and think "I totally misread this".

Final Thoughts

Our mood has plenty of implications on our life. Though our mood is an external representation of our overall mental state, it has its effect on very miniscule aspects of our life to large and macroscopic levels. In the long run, our mood alone can be held responsible for what we have done our whole life—the choices we've made. Though it is really difficult to control our mood, we can always try. Meditating may be one of the possible ways to have our mood on the noose. Because no matter what happens, you wouldn't want your whole life to be an outcome of your emotional impulses would you?

Chapter 21:

5 Ways To Communicate Your Emotional Needs

It's not as easy as it sounds. It's far more challenging to communicate your emotional needs. Especially when you are considered an introvert and are always thinking about others, others always push us back, and we constantly believe not to disappoint or burden them with our emotional needs and wants. That thinking of pleasing others always ends as our loss. Mentally as well as emotionally. One major step towards identifying your goal would be the path of understanding your own emotions first. If you are confused about your feelings, it will be more challenging to reflect them in your actions.

Vulnerability and self-reflection are the main factors to point out your emotions, and that way, it will be easier to show others what you feel. Self-communication is very important in this regard. Think about what you need. Forget about society, family, and friends for a while and start thinking only about what you need or want. Please make sure they are your thoughts without any brainwashing from the outsiders. This way, we will get aware of our own personal and emotional needs. Here are some easier ways to communicate your moving needs.

1. Privacy

A person needs to be wise with their words. Make sure you keep things to yourself as much as possible. It doesn't mean to stay away from people. Right things at appropriate times matter. Keep your point firmly and try not to explain it again and again. Reflect your emotion in your sentence. Make sure others get aware of your feelings just by the way you are talking. Keep things to yourself that are not necessary to discuss with others. Talk with people, be a little outgoing too. The main point is to be careful.

2. Be Confident

You need to make sure that others know what you need. Confidently put up to them. Be rightfully confident to have your needs. Confidence is critical while communicating with someone. People will listen attentively when they know you won't waste their time while being shy and difficult. It would be best if you practiced confidence. It won't come naturally but with time and work. But people will acknowledge your emotional needs when you are confident about them.

3. Observation

People who keep to themselves mostly tend to have an on-point observation about things. If you constantly look at your phone, they will notice that without any unique analysis. When you observe something about someone that disturbs you or affects you mentally somehow, you need to point it out. You need to get that observation in their knowledge so they would know what they are doing wrong. Keeping it to yourself will disturb you even more, and this will continue until they get aware of it any other way. There is possibly less chance that someone else would tell them. So, you have to do it yourself. Take your courage, tell them whatever you think is right. That is a way to communicate your emotional needs to others.

4. Don't Hold The Issues For Too Long

Any issue that occurs in your life needs to be addressed. But if someone is ignorant about it, you need not make them listen again and again. Stop over-explaining. Keep your issue on the table once or twice. If you observe that the other person doesn't get it, then let that issue go entirely. This will save you emotional energy and lots of time. People who care about you will listen to you the first time you complain about something. They would want to work pun that if not, there is nothing more someone can do.

5. Be Open-Minded

Don't close yourself to the world. When something you want needs to be put out there, then be open-minded about it. No matter if it's your relationship, your friendship, or any other association. It would be best if you were open about your emotional needs. Communicate with them so they will know your needs better. If something bothers you, ask questions about it without hesitation. They will take your hesitation as the poor choice of decision when it's just your mind trying to let it go. But that would be against our emotional needs.

Conclusion

We all have our emotional needs and wants. What we need is a way to communicate it with other people. We need to make sure they know how stressful they can get by being ignorant about our needs. Communication is the key to any relationship. Communicating your emotional needs is just as important.

Chapter 22:

5 Scientific Tricks To Become Perfectly Happy

Being happy comes naturally. Almost everything around us makes us happy in a certain way. Being happy is a constant feeling inside a human being. They always tend to get satisfied, even at a minimum. Everywhere we look nowadays, we see things filled with this bright emotion. We tune to the songs written about happiness, we see posters at every corner about being happy, and most importantly, we have people who make us happy. Being happy comes freely, without any fee.

There are scientific ways to become happy because an average human is always looking for more.

Some ways in which you'll feel full at heart and eased at mind. A burst of good laughter is like medicine to the core. So, science has given us ways to take this medicine without and cautions. Being happy is one of the least harmful emotions. It binds people together. Even some forms have been scientifically proven to work in favor of our happiness. There is almost no end to those bright smiles on our lips or those crinkles by our eyes. As it said, smiling is contagious. And we all prefer to smile back at everyone who smiles at us automatically. Here are some scientific ways to be happy.

1. **Minutes Into Exercise**

It is proven that some exercise helps you to smile and laugh more. If there is an exercise to be happy with, then people would be sure to give it a try now and then. Exercise helps us to regulate our jaw muscle, so it will be easier to pass a smile next time. There is also meditation. It enables you to calm your mind and leads towards an easier life. It usually helps to keep you at peace so you'll feel happier towards the things that should make you happy. You'll start to get more content at certain or small items. It becomes a habit slowly to smile more, be more satisfied. Being happy also benefits others, and then they will be more inclined to be pleased towards you.

2. **Get Enough Sleep**

Another scientifically proven way to get happy is to sleep enough every night. It helps with the formation of a proper mindset towards your happiness in life. Sleeping at least 8 hours a day is a must for being happy; if not, the 7 hours would suffice enough for you to smile a little more. It keeps your mind and soul at a steady pace, which is inclined to keep us calm and collected. Keeping calm and organized is one of the factors to be happy. Wake up early to listen to the birds or go for a morning run. Keep yourself fresh in the morning to be a better and happier person. Early to bed is a wise men choice. So, get a sound slumber every night to have a sunny morning following you.

3. Take A Break Now and Then

Even the greatest minds need some rest, so it's only average for a human to get some rest after a long period of working day and night. Go on a vacation. Get a leave because life needs to be enjoyed through anything. Working all the time makes you dull and unhappy. So, make sure to take a break once in a while to start again with a fresh mind and perform a better duty. Don't load yourself with the things that won't matter in a few years. Take vacation so you'll have a more peaceful time ahead of you in your life.

4. Build Your Happy Place

People tend to get tired quickly and often by working all the time. All most of the time, vacation can't seem like an option. So, the best place to visit in such a situation is your happy place—a place you have created in your mind where you are so glad all the time. Just by imagining such a place, you get comfortable and tend to keep working and being pleased with the same time. Your happy place gives you joy, and you become a happier person overall. And it is just easier to carry your vacation with you all the time.

5. Count Your Achievements

A great way to be scientifically happy is to count all the achievements you have made so far. Even count little things like watering plants as an achievement because it gives you a sense of joy. Achievements tell you that you have done more in your life than you intended to, and you will get motivated to do more every time. It makes you believe in yourself and get you going only forwards. You get happy with the deeds you have done till now, and it helps you plan your next good achievement. You naturally become more inclined to fulfill your desires and needs. All the things you have done so far will make you feel beneficial to society and happier for yourself.

Conclusion

Being happy is a great feeling with a more remarkable result in life. So, smiling more won't do you any wrong; in fact, it may be good for you to stretch your jaw a little. Happiness doesn't discriminate, so it will be good to spread this scientific happiness as much as we can. Being happy gives us a sense of undeniable joy and a vision of a positive and bright future.

Chapter 23:

4 Tips For Mindful Self-Compassion

Self-compassion is often a radically new way to relate to yourself. Research shows that the more you practice kindness and self-compassion through informal practices like taking a break or through formal meditation like a gentle breathing, the more self-compassion habits you develop.

Here are some tips for practicing important self-compassion that beginners and experienced meditators should remember. Self-compassion is not about kind feelings; and it's about goodwill. In other words, while a friendly and supportive attitude of self-compassion aims to alleviate suffering, we do not always have control over the situation. The situation will only get worse if we use the practice of self-compassion to suppress or fight off suffering. With self-compassion, we consciously accept painful moments, and in return, we receive ourselves with kindness and concern, remembering that imperfections are part of the overall human experience. It gives us the support and comfort we need to cope with suffering while providing optimal conditions for growth and change and keeps us in love and connected.

1. Self-Kindness

Self-kindness is showing kindness and understanding to ourselves when we fail or suffer. Instead of criticizing or judging ourselves harshly when we are already suffering, we can acknowledge the adverse effects of our self-esteem and instead treat ourselves with warmth and patience—in short, being kind means treating our values unconditionally, even if we fall short of our expectations, whether because of our actions or even our thoughts.

2. Common Humanity

"Being part of the larger" is a prevalent concept in the positive psychology literature, and it has long been argued that the need to connect is part of human nature. Common humanity means viewing our personal experiences as inherent in the broader human experience, not as isolated or separate from others. In part, this accepts and forgives our shortcomings. Although we are imperfect, we show compassion for ourselves when we forgive ourselves for our limitations. Another aspect of humanity, in general, is not only that we are flawed or offended; Instead of isolating or isolating ourselves, we acknowledge that others sometimes feel the same way.

3. Mindfulness

In self-compassion theory, mindfulness is viewed as the opposite of avoidance or over-identification. This involves recognizing and labelling your thoughts rather than reacting to them. We become aware of our painful thoughts and feelings without diminishing their importance through reflection when we have compassion. Instead, we strike a positive balance between excessive identification on the one hand and complete avoidance of painful emotions and worries on the other.

4. Treat Yourself as You'd Treat a Friend

A good starting point is to think about how you treat others you love. So while we cannot permanently alleviate the suffering of others, we can acknowledge the existence of hell and provide support to help them overcome and grow. On this occasion:

Allow yourself to be wrong. Self-kindness and humanity come together as two separate but interconnected ideas. "We are human. But) as well as everyone else. and b) everything is normal." Instead of interpreting our thoughts, feelings, and actions as they are, we can relax when we can do the same to others. If your friend is lazy and doesn't answer the phone, you won't know right away if that friend is the wrong person. Sometimes allowing yourself to be human is one way to acknowledge your flaws and remind yourself that you are not the only imperfect person. Take care of yourself as you treat others. Closely related to the previous tip, what you understand and empathize with. If your friend is depressed, hurt, or upset, you can physically pat him on the back or hold his hand. Neff describes this as a way to connect it to our own "care system." Releases oxytocin, which has beneficial effects on the cardiovascular system. Coupled with soft, modest words (using expressions of affection such as "Baby" or "Honey"), these gestures can make you feel proud, even if you initially resist. Of course, please don't overdo it with cute words unless it looks too weird!

Self-compassion is fundamentally refreshing. It takes a conscious effort to become aware of mental processes initially, but most worthwhile things require practice. We've looked at several different techniques for showing self-compassion regularly, so if writing a letter isn't for you, hopefully, an affirmation or a journal will help.

Chapter 24:

Five Best Psychological Negotiation Tactics

The Power of Negotiation

Negotiation is the process of reaching a compromise. We may not agree on everything with other people but there could be some level of agreement. Negotiation has abetted wars, calmed down tensions, and even built trust between people. It unlocks a myriad of opportunities. Not anybody can initiate negotiations. Some may try and cause more harm than the good intended. Negotiation is not a pedestrian skill. It is a psychological one that requires aptness. The role of psychology in negotiation is the greatest. You have to find a way around it to succeed in negotiations. Here are five of the best psychological negotiation tactics:

1. **Calmness**

Calmness is not only a state but also a tactical lifestyle. It is the ability to be still, physically, and emotionally, even when you are provoked. What do we say about the weather when it is calm? We observe the trees to see whether it is windy. Of course, it is difficult to be calm, but the general stillness of trees indicates calm weather. This is the relationship between calmness and psychology: not being swayed by emotions, from yourself or other people, when in negotiation talks. Maintain calm and do not stake anything during negotiations when you are emotional. Probably the gospel of following your heart has reached you too. There is a caution here – it does not apply during negotiations. Always let logic prevail.

2. Appeal To The Other Person's Self-Interest

Negotiations involve two or more parties. This tactic infers that you are not selfish during negotiations. You must be prepared to compromise on a few things. For successful negotiations, do not let your self-interests overtake the discussions. Do your homework very well of knowing what interests the other person holds. This information is useful during negotiation. Find a way of reaching a compromise that will take care of their interests. They will quickly accept your offer.

3. Conceal Your Intentions

In his best-selling book, *the 48 laws of power*, Robert Greene talks about this law – **Conceal your intentions.** Take this in mind before you enter into any form of negotiations. It is good to have an open mind but in doing so, do not be fast to reveal your intentions. Take your time to understand the one(s) sitting at the other end of the table. You are disadvantaged when they read your intentions before you know theirs. Do not have secrets when negotiating because the other person(s) will feel shortchanged and your talks will be unfruitful. Negotiation happens in stages. Do not empty everything at once.

4. Show Genuine Concern

Genuine concern is important during negotiation. You do not have to use words like *"I understand how you are feeling."* It is being insensitive to the other person's feelings because they are the only ones who understand what they are feeling at the moment. Do not rub their pain on their face as much as you are trying to relate to their pain. Negotiations are delicate especially when it involves emotions. You can easily misrepresent facts, and this can undo any progress you may have made.

5. Create A Win-Win Outcome

Nobody wants to be on the losing side, even if they rightfully deserve it. When at negotiations, do not make it a winning affair. By all means, avoid the competition part. It is more of an understanding than it is a competition. At the end of the talks, make the other person also feel part of the process and a winner too. Do not take credit alone for anything. Let it be a **we** affair rather than an **I**.

Conclusion

The beauty of negotiations is when a consensus is arrived at. Find a way of reading the mind of the other person and act appropriately. These five psychological negotiation tactics will take you there.

www.ingramcontent.com/pod-product-compliance
Lightning Source LLC
Chambersburg PA
CBHW072102110526
44590CB00018B/3281